Beati

1999

Beatitudes of Ice

poems by

Rienzi Crusz

TSAR
Toronto
Oxford
1995

The publishers acknowledge generous assistance from
The Ontario Arts Council and the Canada Council.

Cover art and design by Virgil Burnett
*The illustration shows the soft, almost voluptuous features of the
Indian Ocean person (chin, lips), hidden by the Mask and Costume
of Europe (Venetian half-mask, high stiff collar, tattered neckcloth), and
the headdress or wig is invaded by forms (claws, fangs) from the
Animal Underworld lurking in every culture.*
—VB

Author photograph by Jerome Crusz

Canadian Cataloguing in Publication Data

Crusz, Rienzi, 1925-
  Beatitudes of ice

Poems.
ISBN 0-920661-51-3

I. Title.

PS8555.R87B4 1995   C811'.54   C95-932508-5
PR9199.3.C78B4 1995

Printed and bound in Canada

TSAR publications
P. O. Box 6996, Station A
Toronto, Ontario M5W 1X7
Canada

PRAISE FOR RIENZI CRUSZ'S POETRY:

If you want to share a sensibility which is at once primitive and
sophisticated, both intense and subtle, a poetic craft which is taut
and concentrated, then read *Flesh and Thorn*.   *Quarry*

Can Lit . . . has never articulated and transcended the experience of
the incomer so wonderfully . . . the voice rings with a timbre
known at once and altogether distinct; its range is abnormally
large; its tone of infinite variety.   *The New Quarterly*

The cultural gift Crusz offers us, as a kind of magnificent verbal em-
broidery of the plain cloth of Canadian speech, continually
surprises, delights, mystifies and liberates those of us raised on the
sound of what Northrop Fry has called "the Canadian goose honk."
                              The Toronto South Asian Review

Arguably the best living Sri Lankan poet in English, though he has
been in Canada since 1965, Crusz belongs to that older post-
colonial generation, including such writers as Walcott and Soyinka,
prepared to appropriate the colonial legacy of Shakespeare and
English without anguished breast beating, "as a tongue to speak
with."   *World Literature Today*

His "Immigrant's Song" is not only an attempt to come to terms
with his own past, it is also a heroic statement of poetic
independence.   Arun Mukherjee, *Currents*

Crusz, the most delicately nuanced (of such voices) uses his to balance a history, a role, and a difficult displacement . . . Like the West Indian poet, Derek Walcott [he] will not indulge in simplified opposition, whether of language, culture or colour. *Ariel*

Crusz's language is subtle and he makes his points obliquely. Moreover, his self-examination always includes the social context of an immigrant's struggle for a sense of identity.   *Books in Canada*

The Sun-Man poems are major artifacts of a new Canadian sensibility, important for the realities of our national selfhood.
                    Nancy Lou Patterson, University of Waterloo

Here was a true poetry of the displaced self, with sorrow beneath its bemused surface. Opposites—elephant and ice—are reconciled by a delightful wit, and ferocious though may be his interior heat, the light that the Sun-Man sheds upon the world lingers in the mind with a lovely after-glow.
                    Zulfikar Ghose, University of Texas

To call Crusz an immigrant poet is to summarize his intents too glibly. In both his books it is not the obvious contrast between elephant and ice, Sri Lanka and Canada, that is central but rather the manifold and specific ways in which a certain sensibility tries to cope honestly with perennial themes in both cultures.
                    Reshard Gool

A most articulate poetry, with a fascinating sense of where you come from and where to.   Robert Creely

His real genius lies not in the message contained in the poetry, but in the pursuit of perfection in poetic form. Very much a poet of sound and rhythm, Crusz writes with an awareness that poetry is about language, about the power of imagination. He is a very self-conscious poet, and that is precisely why his reputation will outlast that of his contemporaries.
                    Chelva Kanaganayakam, University of Toronto

In memory
of that beloved and saintly troubleshooter
Fr Justin Perera

Out of profound silence, something like
a chorus soft and grand,
longing, soars to the terrace where I stand:
and in redolence of laurel,
of laurel langourous, laurel piercing, where
those statues in the sunset loomed immortal,
she appears, present there.

Dino Campana

ACKNOWLEDGEMENTS

Some of these poems first appeared in the following journals:

*The Malahat Review, Possibilitiis, The Toronto South Asian Review,
Fiddlehead, Ariel, The Toronto Review, The New Quarterly,
The South Asian Review* (University of Michigan), *Prism International*.

I thank the Canada Council, the Department of Canadian Heritage,
Multicultural Programs for financial assistance in writing this book;
also, the Ontario Arts Council for various grants.

CONTENTS

4   *For the Passionate Ones*

1

A Sky of My Own

Leave him in his garden, so secluded,
where like angels he would welcome you
on those paths he daily wandered through,
by those waiting seats where shadows brooded,
in there where the lute hung leave him too.

Rainer Maria Rilke

SEASONS OF MEMORY

Autumn   the apple tree:
just apples, expected, and on time.

Then winter
and nakedness:

wedding blossoms, the sun strobing,
the red fruit

Summer   the green, green grass
is everywhere and nowhere, no,

only castles of snow and Michael
with apple cheeks

drags his toboggan across the lawn,
one eye steady on the snowman   patient,

for his button eyes,
the sculptor's return.

Spring   and the mind
shuttles backwards and forwards:

Morning   the deck laid out,
bacon and eggs.

Evening   a crackling fire,
sherry, Chopin on the keys,

and somebody is crossing the median,
for the 401 to run again with stain.

When there's no emptiness,
for the mind to invade,

when the eyes see and don't
we have a season's configuration,

expected, ordinary.

AFTER THE SNOWFALL

Through garage door lookouts,
winter–hazed:

bleached bones   the catalpa
(without   its green crinoline head)

King maple   so humbled
frail white arms   skying

a tree
praying for its life

Driveway   divided
snow walls   on either side

the Red Sea   parted again
and Moses   nowhere in sight

But Pharaoh   on his snowplough
continues history: walls the last exit,

laughs: there shall be no diaspora today!

O Lord, mine are summer eyes—
tomorrow   the promised land?

your Egypt   still shimmers and shines
in its white   misery

[handwritten annotations:] · speaks about Canada. the promised land.
‾all art breaks away from the past. ‾ when he returns to the past - it's not nostalgia - it's poetic contrast.

4

FROM SHOVEL TO SELF–PROPELLED SNOWBLOWER: THE IMMIGRANT'S PROGRESS

(debilitating years of religious strife)

Two days into the promised land
and my eyes dance:
supermarket and mall,
those shopping faces thick with neon,
plastic cards breathing under their breasts.
One block, and the Golden Ox rises
with Molson froth and snaking smoke,
afternoon men angular in beer laughter.

- accomadation with land
- religious metaphors with respect demanded by ice.
- normal discourse of dreariness
- engaged found in Cruz not present in Espinet

I am in TV's arms,
laugh with the Honeymooners,
the Cuban and his Lucy,
trace blood along the Fugitive's trail.
No one mentioned the forecast: tomorrow
100% precipitation/ freezing rain.
So down the shimmering street I go
with only my sun head and Adidas,
to learn how the feet suddenly slide,
shudder with instant pain,
the body lumps to horizontal woe,
three broken ribs, some hefty pain,
I've learnt the beatitudes of ice,
something sacred, something cold,
demanding respect, a paraphernalia
of horned boots, cowl and padded vest
for body nicely flexed to winter's mould.

After twenty winters in my bones,
shovelling my sidewalk snow,
a self-propelled snowblower I've called Pablo,
now does my chores,
and I'm happy
vertical as my front door.

TIME

Time now ticking
is mere process,
history without verdict;
the uncertainties of pain,
the sick man neither well nor dead,
or the havocking wounds
of the killing fields
without a hint of victory.

Time in passing
is no match
for time past or time to come:
one holds history
like a sacrament, maps
directions, minefields
that will collect the foolish
and the damned. The other,
a hope, a promise
for the blood to surge, race
towards some new Jerusalem.

SUMMERTIME AT WATERLOO PARK

This day was unlike any other day,
the sun went wild
shook the grey morning
by the scruff
and cracked the lingering
winter crystals from my eyes
to a yellow pantomime
of summer people.

There was Lisa,

the pink girl with sun hair,
choking on a blue popsicle;
And Patsy's brown baby
strapped the sun on her back
and bounced
into the round wading pool
with sparrow wings
and duckling feet;
a hush of narrowed eyes,
as Mrs Donova's daughter
shivered the diving board
with velvet heels
and sprang like a sunflower
of olive flesh
to the waiting sun;
Old Mr Rogers was still alive,
and seemed to climb down slowly
from palaces of distant eyes
to green bikini earth;
even Mrs Jones could not be kept out
on a day like this:
she ambled like a pink elephant,
sipping soda through a straw
and thrusting the years
with cracked skin
and redundant muscle.

On the far side,
the old greying park bench
bloomed to the boiled sweating faces
of Mr McIver's family,
their russet mounds
of hot dogs, ketchup, and drumstick chicken
fast disappearing
under their red mouths.

The robins weren't there.

MOVING

When it happens,
and your rooms are finally empty
and bare as bones,   ·
and it's time to step out
from that old ship of sleep,
of dreams,
where you wrote your history
for twenty years and laughed:
    a child sitting on his potty
    pummelling his teddy bear,
    the pappadams hissing and sizzling,
    where buryani and chicken curry
    seduced your Christmas mouths,
    and Santa Claus lumped himself
    on a kitchen chair and went for
    the brandy and eggnog.

What do you say?
What do you keep?

You must know
that the silence of emptiness
is no silence,
it is a wordless thunder,
the hammers of the heart beating
with long-ago laughter,
or stories grave and grieved.

So do not look back
and mourn the moving hour.
What is bare and empty
remains bare and empty
only if the mind lets go
the continuing dream, refuses
memory   history
sitting on the porch at evening
and taking in the evening star.

THEATRE OF THE DEAD

No, not Judgement Day,
just another night at

Bechtel Cemetery;
graves   a blur.
The fog lifts,
          shapes
like muslin togas stagger out;

like a mob under gunfire
          they scatter,
converge, hold hands, move
their filaments of bones
round and round:

          ring a ring of roses,
          pocket full of posies. . .

Something huge
raves and rants   jumps
from headstone to headstone:

          "Here lies the slob
          who only loved himself,
          his beer and his dog.
          May he rest with them for ever.
          Love. Maggie"

I see pain
in the eyeless hollows,
wolflike, the way
it raised the headstone
over its head
and crashed its story
into the graveyard dirt .

Something crawls sideways

like a sandcrab,
a yellow froth spilling
through its ear bones:
"Where's my gin, where's my gin?"
it screams, the face
an alcoholic grimace.

It was rumoured
that someone had bought
his own cemetery plot years ago
and buried 25 bottles of Gordon's
for future use.

About to leave,
          symphony :
sweet trombones, violins, guitars,
cymbals   baila drums.
The white things break into song,
dip and sway, shadowy bones
in perfect rhythm.

And then   cock's crow
and they suddenly freeze, scurry
like prairie dogs   back
into their graves.

What were these hours
of birthing dawn ?

The hours of Carnivaal,
the spirit made flesh ?

LATE EVENING IN THE BECHTEL WOODS

Show me
where the woods begin

and I'll pass
the park's vaulted blue skies

the baseball stadium's raucous laughter
the thin voices that race down the matslides,

rise and fall
to the happy arcs of the swings.

Into this narrow path
that opens into a kingdom:

tall trees, close as lovers,
breathe on each other,

talk
in rustling vocabularies.

I see an autumn leaf unhinge,
separate from its mother,

fall back to the womb, golden,
to return in due season.

Scrubgrass, weeds
hug my ankles like friendly imps,

the fallen leaves
soft refuge for my sore feet.

As twilight stains
the last sliver of light through the trees,

darkness tiptoes in like a thief,

and my eyes, my ears, magnify

the fragile dusk
to a midnight ghost,

the thin silence
to a sweet thunder:

the bedtime chatter of birds,
up safe in their feathered boudoirs.

SONG FOR THE BURNING BUSH

Gone the way of all seasons
winter's cold hand,

and you without hint
or prophecy of fire.

What flame from scrawny arms, anorexic trunk,
whose sap now trickling down to its toes,

    holds life above ground
    in some cruel shape of death?

Why the crocus
has already cracked a season,

the tulip fevered   ready
for its opening riot,

But you, still cold and grey,
a noduled blur.

Summer's swarming sun,
and the forsythia leaps ,

the catalpa   opens out
its perfect umbrella,

and you   a green shape,
dull as scrub grass.

Then autumn,
and how your green leaves unravel

the prophecies of fire:
day by day the faint vermilion grows,

deeper and deeper until
you become what you were born to be—

enough
to bring another Moses to his knees.

THE OPPOSITE MEN

Once, sleep came easily
(without Sominex or Sleepeze)

Darkness fermented our dreams, traced
the brilliant vein of stars.

The bat excelled in its blind journeys,
we kept to the paths of light.

Now we ransack night's silent bowl
with torch and headlamp, the pencil light of thieves,

disco drums, beered tongues,
engines coughing along our highways.

From night, we make the raw hunk of a Vegas day,
from day, we learn to sleep in the hairy arms of the sloth.

We who are fat, hunger to be thin,
the thin gorge themselves for bulk and curve.

We who are proud as stallions
seek loincloth and ashes for a single faddish day,

And we who have no bread
demand Angel Cake.

We are the opposite men,
found West when we should be East, North when South,

like Adam, caught again,
with the contrary apple in our mouth.

CITY WITHOUT A NAME

An immigrant city   waits   *city full of hope to be (re)defined*
for a name.

The City Council debates
into the deep night, wee hours
as autumn stars lose their fevers.
And still   confusion,
raw nerves, tempers feeding
on sleepy eyes.

What name
for this plexus of colour, culture, language?
Part heaven, part hell,
some purgatory, some limbo;
part white, part black,
brown, yellow, and in between:

palm trees, mynah birds,
elephants trumpeting from open verandas;
red cement floors, ayahs
with brown babies laughing
in their arms,
where the bougainvillea explodes,
the shoeflower is colour.

Here steel drums zing,
as the calypso beat pulses through the city
like a heart;
Rum and Coca-Cola, Carnivaal,
and a thousand joyous imps
jump the city streets;
Where Mayaro beach is jewel
basking in the sun
and Ibis and immortelle leap
from their habitats like fire.

Where the snow falls silently

like a prayer,
and the snowman   waits patiently
for its maker;
how daring men speak
to cold and squall, a winter storm
with parkas and studded boots,
a mind that deflects
a season's rage.

What name
for a city with the world in its arms ?

MEMORY'S TRUTH

I've left the green land,

        mother country—
So, what thoughts
            will ever silence

memory to be interrogated, debated, contested as not permanent
memory is malleable.

the infant footfalls
        on red cement floors,
restore the omphalos blood
            that sang my green days?

How argue the diaspora?

        Would I let nostalgia
flirt with hyperbole?
        Is there enough love
to conjure past perfections,
            forget, forgive
those strident voices,
    the arrythmia of the wicked heart?

Son born in Canada on p. 21.

16

I know. I'll make the coconut tree
            forever straight,
without hint of midnight beetle   deep
      in the pink fruit's throat.

There's a raging moon,
                  the fruit bat's nightly orgy is on;
but cadju pulang and mango
                  will still be whole and sweet
as newborn toddy—
            Nothing will fester
under this extravagant sun,
                  the fruit fly will not feast.

As for the monsoon rain,
                  there'll only be the beautiful slant
of raindrops,
            cool massage,
me dancing naked
                  under God's own shower head;
And the havocking floods,
                  mud huts dissolving like chocolate?
bloated bodies
            riding the dark currents to the sea?

I wouldn't know.

From here,
            this imperfect beautiful land,
new entrances seem
                  rational, imperative;
old exits survive, ride
                  the sweet inventions of memory;
the green land
            forever green,
the lost country
            ever perfect.

2

Distant Rain

The mind, that ocean where each kind
Does straight its own resemblance find;
Yet it creates, transcending these,
Far other worlds and other seas,
Annihilating all that's made
To a green thought in a green shade

Andrew Marvell

RICE

Michael,
it's time to let go:
mother's milk, those other founts
that spread like water
at your roots.
But don't talk of pablum,
or ask for Heinz or Gerber's,

ask for the ceremonies
of rice,   soft-boiled,
Lanka's first and solid sequel
to mother's milk.

When you enter the heart
of the paddies, you enter
the mouths of your fathers,
a nation, continents,
half the world (living and breathing
in a grain of rice)

And you'll grow strong
and straight as a coconut tree.
Look at you,
how the paddies
have fulfilled their promise;
how you love the taste of Basmati,
the Samba grains, distinct and separate
as pearls.

But now,
up here in snow land,
you have turned against rice,
embraced the wiener between the bun,
some dog called "hot,"
a mouthful of yellow chips,
salted, serrated, barbecued;

·interesting statement
of generational
differences.

21

I watch the fries disappear
in your mouth like quicksand;
your daily ritual
of hamburgers (with everything on it)
spread their juice down your shirt,
your new-found throat.

Son,
somewhere in the paddy lands,
a farmer still gives his bare back
to the cruel sun,
the buffalo, their thick wearied legs
to the plough,
and the mud furrows will again
sprout the paddies

to feed a world
that you know no more.

DISTANT RAIN

Your exotic pot
of White Rose hibiscus
has never known the Island sun
or monsoon rain.
So memory for you, my son,
is without green history.

As glass and stone
have framed your dark eyes
and all you know
is that land that falls asleep
in soft white pyjamas
with snow flakes to muffle
its heavy breathing,
I guess you'll keep on
asking angrily:
do you have to hang up your story   *past of father, present*
like a butcher's side of beef?   *of son*
Why another poem?
Why roll the rock
from the mouth of the tomb,
what's there in shadows, dry bones,
memories ?

I raise my tired eyes
from the title of a poem
still new, fierce and lamenting:
"The Rain Doesn"t Know Me Any More."
        To remember, to remember
the raindrops
bigger than my childhood eyes,
those blue fists
fast and liquid as a therapist's.

How the good earth churned
its red dust bowl,
burgeoned to batik profusion,

and the sky caught the colours below
like a memory.

YOU CANNOT TELL ME THAT I'M NOT AN ELEPHANT

You cannot tell me
that I'm not an elephant

because I stood apart from the herd,
spilled my elegy in whispers
and trumpeted the last post for a dying bull;
the magic of my memory,
how I trampled my mahout to death
for a ten-year-old harassing word, unkind prod.

Because I often lie on my back
with my thick legs vertical
to the Serengeti stars;
make music (instead of
the hyena's murderous bark)
whenever I call to the sensuous moon
as it rides over the Acacia tree.

Because I can blow smoke
through my trunk,
play the mouth organ,
swivel on a wooden stool
two feet in diameter,
pick a pin from a haystack
with the magnet of my nose.

You cannot tell me
that I'm not an elephant.

Because I am wise

in the ways of water,
smell a waterhole miles across the plains,
can dig a life-saving well with my bare tusks;
because I sleep standing
without ever rolling over,
with only my big ears flapping
in the night breeze.

Because it seems odd to you
that my great bulk
can ride on leaf and woodapple,
the sweet bark that fights desperately
to stay with its tree like a body suit;
because I can talk to my family
twenty miles away
with a voice beyond and below the human ear.

You cannot tell me
that I'm not an elephant.

Because I know the pain
in the sound of the chains,
the harassing voice   dream
of green Africa, the virgin forests,
the waterhole that once gathered the great herds
as if for a common baptism.

Because I know
the time of my going
(when the bicuspids in my mouth
have sunk beneath my gums
and I can no longer chew the sweet bark
or stem of leaf)
and my old legs take me as in dream
to the graveyard of my brothers.

SILVERFISH

The long night.
    Silence
heavy as midsummer air.
    The sweet papers   scream
and no one hears.
    Silverfish salivating,
feeding on their gourmet meal.

Dust. Unmoved. Congealed.
    How cruel design rides on dampness,
the unholy dark, an appetite
    for the flavours
that glaze the words of poets,
    long dead and famous.

Nothing escapes
    the bristly tail,
the long feelers,
    the microbe teeth,
the gut that grows
    with the colour of night.

"It's the damn climate," he would swear,
    my father's ears red as beet.
"Too hot, too humid,
too damn tropically dark
    for literature, philosophy,
immortal words;
    what to do but dust and wait,
wait for the next onslaught.

What do these microbe killers know
    of Thomas A Kempis ?
His holy commandments
    now broken with absent words,
vowels, meanings plucked like summer fruit;
    O Bard of Avon, forgive, forgive,

your pillaged text, I know
  mad Hamlet spoke more eloquently than this;
and where are the opening lines
  of the Hound of Heaven?
Why they now sit as pablum
  in the insect's belly."

"Dampness. Darkness. Bloody Silverfish. Death."
  Words
my father always muttered to himself
  like some congenital idiot.
How he would often hang his head
  and ask: "Why this cruel conspiracy
on silver scales ?
  Why sweet literature
hobo now in tattered clothes?"

SYNTHESIS

Bird: round red breast,
strutting on spring grass.
The natives call it a robin.
I call it a paddy bird.

— naming of bird exercise.
Synthesizing the two.

Bird: black with yellow beak,
head fashioned for talking.
The natives call it a mynah bird.
You call it a blackbird.

Somewhere in this confusion
of feather, beak and name,
lies a meaning, a name
that's not ornithological
but true,

like the sun
that fuses East and West
in one embracing journey,
each bird has only
one real name,

that which nestles
in the comfort of the eyes,
the mind.

CONNECTIONS

5:20 AM, and why
does the old gardener suddenly see
a horizon of golden orioles
in the October sky?
Hear, Baba, the zoo elephant,
trumpet over the ramparts of Galle?
It's the father   whistling,
as he slips out of the womb,
and claps wildly
at the midwife's magic manipulations.

*home is not home
of Sri Lankan cousins*

Mother
makes her grand entrance
with a yell and a song,
a kaffrinja rhythm
that swells over the banks of the Kelaniya,
here ravens pick up the news
in one happy chorus,
and fishermen go out to sea
as if a Biblical catch
is heavy in the wind.

Black clouds drift discreetly
from out of a cold February moon,
make way
for a coming;
the taxi driver holds his Capuchin silence
as the new snow dogs the mother's trail
to the KW Hospital like a ghost.

And a son is born,
loud and feisty,
brown as chocolate,
with fists quick as a champion's,
enough, for the nurse to remark:
"We have a beautiful,
something-else baby today!"

Come summer
and the family is back
to its sun beginnings;
suck the sweet rambuttan,
let the mango juice run down your shirt;
watch the zoo elephants
as they perilously walk over
the prostrate bodies of their mahouts
without a crack of bone.

Do you hear the Perahera drums,
the thump and anklet bells
of the Kandyan dancers ?
Can you take in Kasyappa's mountain kingdom
where fresco queens smile
from their rock boudoirs ?
Come Michael,
make friends with your Sri Lankan cousins,
greet your uncles and aunts, talk,
talk with everyone, enjoy yourself,

this is the land of your fathers!

Nothing stirs. He moves clumsily
in air thick as fog.
Hates the language.
Hates the mud and dirt,
dog shit drying in the sun,
those other monsoon leavings.

There's a tempest in his eyes:
the snow swirls, coagulates.
He conjures a shimmering white landscape,
hears the call of the snow goose,
is happy
for the bluejay and robin   scrounging
in his backyard.

Home is where the snowman

- home and homeland
Narrative logic of
diaspora.

Child's mother
tongue is another
language.

sits on the front lawn
and waits patiently
for his return.

Son named Michael.

THE WORD MADE GOOD

High noon.
The Plantation sags   sweats
under Haputale's mauling sun.
The bloodsucker on the lawn
is pure sculpture, the rosebud
a phantasmagoria of blood.

In the Superintendent's bungalow,
siesta holds the Englishman stiff
on his divan, his eyes folded.
The veranda barely hides the servants
drooping
like flowers in a vase.

Not for long—
the master's voice booms
at a bare-bodied man
standing arrogant
at the door, his rifle
catching the afternoon sun
through the window like a mirror.

"Who are you ?
What the hell do you want?"
"I am Sardiel of Uttuwankande.
I want 131 rupees immediately,
not a cent more or less.
Will you lend me the money, Sir ?"

"Yes, but why this exact amount ,
and why demand such a paltry sum
at the point of a gun?"

"Today, as the half-moon
crawls over the Rock,
I need to pay my debt to Carolis,
a poor villager. Monies borrowed
(also at the point of a gun)
for my gambling at cards.
Sardiel of Uttuwankande
always keeps his word."

He is last seen
on his knees   bending over
to smell the roses.

Stunned servants crowd the divan,
the head appu protesting:
    "Master doing foolish thing.
    Big rogue this Sardiel,
    very dangerous man, too.
    Master should call police."

" No. Have you heard the name 'Robin Hood' ?"

Bungalow gossip
hardly two days old,
when a hulking man stands at the front door,
hands the houseboy a large package.
Rolled in leopard's skin
is the Englishman's rifle,
the servant's sword,
and a crocodile skin
bulging with 131 rupees!

SENTIMENTAL JOURNEY

Where the mind would seem
to turn away from the mind,
the heart's blood rushes
to a new rhythm;
where everything is for the eye,
and the eye is everything:

How a crow makes new geometry
under a shimmering shower of rain,
caws and caws and caws
as if pleading ;
what happens at evening
when our coolie bird squats
under the jambu tree,
all dressed up for dinner.

And this flooded rice-paddy field
where the water hyacinths now thrive
like summer grass,
a lone heron, quiet as a Buddha,
balances on one chopstick leg,
and a fishing crane skims the waters,
sees nothing but his own thin shadow.

Shoreline,
cadjan huts crouch
against the wind,
and sunburnt fishermen
froth at the mouth, coconut toddy,
as their fat nagging wives,
scalliwag children, pariah dogs
bask in the sun
like metaphors of misery.

Then magic: the Dehiwela Zoo:
We have acrobats,
a mouth organ ensemble,

mahouts with only a prod
and a mantara word
moving tons of flesh
to a delicate dance.

This land of the eternal summers:
blue fists of rain
for cruel winter,
where the grass grows wildly green,
and no one sees
the jaundiced shambles of autumn.

There is no death here,
no beginning   no end,
only the everlasting effusion,
the green blessing of the sun.

(Colombo, Sri Lanka, July 1993)

3

Song of Myself

(with apologies to Walt Whitman)

I am not Theocritus: I took hold of life
and faced her and kissed her until I subdued her,
and then I went through the tunnels of the mines
to see how other men live

Pablo Neruda

. . . but seek the road that makes death
a fulfillment . . .

DAG HAMMARSKJOLD

I will not talk seriously of grief,
or the stabbing moment, or pain
that trickles like blood from under my door.
These I have known,
but unprofitably diagnosed
as ugly transients: crows
that permute common dark moods,
angular flights unworthy of netting,
toads croaking for the havoc of monsoon rain
that never happened.

But take this mango leaf,
once a soft green vein of sap
for the honey fruit, a camouflage
styled for safe summer ripening.

Now, cleanly autumned, scarlet,
at the foot of its mother tree,
with the sun veiling its small architecture
like a tabernacle,
and the tree smiling at its roots
for a death
so exotically done.

SONG OF MYSELF

How you carved the perfect heart
from raw unseasoned wood,
revealed the dark meat
of the new Caesars, grieved
for the wobble and limp
of small men walking
under cold colonnades;

Used words
to match an embracing kiss,
close a vein,
probe an adamant eyelid,
salve the pain
in a throbbing nerve;

Named the fire
of the undressed sun, the fever
in the eyes of immigrant men;
sang loudly
of elephant and ice, children
pulsing through a continent of snow,
the eagle hovering
in its ether currents.

But have you shared
the pain
in the shattered bird,
the silence
of the thorn that guards the rose?

ONLY BECAUSE WE ARE COMING TO THE BEND

Accepting
with cold
locked teeth
the river mud
leap and croak
of bullfrog
battling
for mate
the sun
wilting
in the wounded
dark under
roots drunk
with the salt
of bulrushes

a shapeless
black rock
cracking the water's
brackish pane

a half-moon
of bank
breathing
poisoned trees

and overhead
a raven
wintering
sky and bone
with the city's
fresh garbage

Only because
we are coming to the bend
that opens out
like a soft hand

to the blue
of lagoon
with palms
that hold
pink coconuts
to their breasts

to the sun dance
on the kingfisher's
blue wing
on faces
of green stone
where the sunfish
bask naked
like jewels

and a new sky
from a deep blue bowl
slaking our Sahara mouths
with the lemonade
of summer

SLOW DANCING

For Kingsley

When I stagger each morning into the promise of the day,
sit patiently till the going of the sun;

When I see no stories, revelations, fireflies
in night's hard shadows;

When the city's noonday glare
gives up nothing but hobo clothes, a teen's unloved eyes;

When I pump the heart every fourth hour
with Maxwell House coffee,

and swear by God
on Vitamin E, and B-complex;

When the headlines in my newspaper
seem like old hat,

and I keep to the ads for topsoil,
handymen, tree cutters, and window washers;

When my once dancing feet no longer hear
the tango's gypsy rhythm, the kaffrinja beat,

and I take to the shuffle's slow exertions,
a music plucked from Welk's cotton candy bag;

When like a prayer the menu
comes up with fish and veggies and no dead meat,

and the fridge holds the Heavenly Hash
like forbidden fruit;

When the kneecaps are worn, the eyes crucible,
and the Kingdom of God is at hand,

then know this, my friend,

I'm in the twilight of my bones,

slow dancing.

HOURGLASS

You know me, Lord,
in the hourglass of my breathing.
I know you
in your words, your artifacts.

You say, love,
and the face of God
weeps out of the mirror
as if I were a part of the nightmare;
so the Samaritan listens
to the cries in the havocking alley,
and I take to the dank streets
with coffee for hands shaking
out of cardboard shacks.

You say, hate,
and yes I see Lucifer
warming his hands
over a dark hellfire, screaming
for a sheaf of light
from the seraphim world;
and I am at it again
planning my ugly menus
of revenge and hate,
how to spin the world
round my cynical dreams.

You say, sing,
and violins coax in
the waking light,

noon   the drums,
twilight   sweet serapina,
night   hot seraglio, Lambada,
then utter sleep   silence.

How my world shuttles like a raven
between love, song and hate:
bird now magnificent scythe
against the sun,
now mourning in sweet chorus
for its dead,
then contradictory
as it fouls the siesta air,
or unfurls the skull and bones,
live meat dying in its adamant beak.

Who said the raven
is only shaped to a strident caw,
a sack of black bones
without language or meaning or metaphor?
Who said the bird is beyond poetry,
the hourglass under God?

LISTENING TO THE RAVEN

For Stephan

The winter bird keeps its silence
like some mountain fakir,

so you turn to the seducing music
of the womb and sleep.

With spring's sweet twitter,
new robin on the lawn,

you begin to gurgle, swim joyously,
in your warm amniotic sea.

Chicadees hail the morning light,
and you're hampster on ferris wheel,

and as the catalpa slowly undresses in the wind,
the king maple loses its crown,

you stretch and curl and kick,
just to say that you're ready for new beginnings.

And when, soon after, you think
you've heard the raven caw,

church bells
through the autumn air,

you come out lustily,
your primordial song   ricocheting

from your mother's glistening eyes
to a world   waiting

for another miracle.

44

DISCOVERY

What if I call you
the great impostor, the perfect decoy,
the one who (as the poet said)
quietly throws a bomb into the crowd,
walks calmly away
to reach for his notebook?

Who are these imps
that perch on my shoulder
like acrobats, that fashion
my tableaux of slow pain?
And you laughing
as another man
drains his dream away,

and a woman plays out her life
like a child with her broken dolls.
God, the mischief in his pariah eyes,
tricks so carefully tucked under
his sleeves like a magician.

And why the maze
of these many years ?
this karma
where each turn was another turn,
the pain of lost roads, directions
moving away from the sun.
Give me a path
not to my green beginnings,
but to myself:

Who needs the green fields
that now crackle with fallen bones,
bridges   burning, flaming tires
as crowns of death,
the clinking irons ready
for the new politics?

No more: the nightmare silhouettes,
laughter at the flotsam clothes
on an old man's back, hurt
that heaves under his shoulder blades
like an accordion;
no more   the silence,
the throat that would not cry
for all its pain.

Enough of smoke and edges,
parry and thrust;
I'm well into the ugly truth
of your face, the fires
that burned my sun years,
the lies
that fashioned an idiot mind.

Impostor   substance
always separates from shadow,
the heart forever distinct
from peripheral muscle;
as the decoy steals away,
the real game moves in,

and I hear noises,
the chatter of imps
spill from my own mouth,
a black heart beating, beating
in me like thunder,

like the heart,
is the heart
of all my pain.

THE SUN-MAN TAKES A TATTOO

At the Turtle Tattoo Shoppe,
the Sun Man asks Donnae, the tattoo man,
to wound his brown skin in three places:
　Lay it on good, Donnae,
　and in flaming color:
　on my chest the Christ's head,
　my left arm,
　a Valentine's heart,
　cracked four ways;
　my right,
　a baby laughing through a blue soother.

And what does it all mean?
asks the tattoo man.
　Don't ask for answers,
　ask for history: the pain   *– wound as corporial metaphor.*
　of my woundings, the diaspora   *Sri Lankan in Toronto.*
　that runs through my life   *first wave of migration came*
　like an alphabet.   *before multicultural theory hit*
　　canada.   under-
　　-assimilist ethos pins the poems.

And how do I nurse
these Christ-like wounds?   *as one *Cruz has been referred to*
Keep these signatures for ever?   *of the finest poets.*
　Remove the bandage in one hour.   *Cruz's writing is founda-*
　If it sticks, soak it off, don't pull it.   *tional. Diasporic sensibility*
　Bathe tattoos in cold water to remove dry blood.   *–Attempt to transcend*
　Use only specified ointment. Apply lightly.   *slaughting of post-*
　Extended soaking in hot water is not advised.   *colonial, diasporic,*
　If scabbing occurs, do not scratch or pick.   *migrant, etc.*
　Above all, keep the tattoos clean.   *–even as events in*
　　another country function
　　as informative, poem
Christ! swears the Sun-Man,   *suggest engagement*
and the crucified tattoo on his chest   *with poetic meanings*
winces again
like the Jesus of old.   *– working to larger*
　　feelings of poetic agenda

　　　　(23 January 1994)

Sometimes to be silent is to lie.
                    MIGUEL DE UNAMUNO

Gone the mint jujubes
from her candy jar,
and grandma foams at the mouth.
The whole household suspect:
anyone of us could have killed
for the likes of a mint jujube.

Truth begs for declarations,
or at least some story
from the muscles of my face,
or the language of my eyes,
but I nurse my silence like a Buddha.

Imagine the thrill of the steal,
the phantom footsteps, the timing
between grandma's regular dozings;
the jujubes melting,
melting too soon, too soon,
my mouth in the aftertaste of mint.

Christmas eve, 2:00 A.M,
and I catch grandpa tiptoeing
down the stairs, trying
to play Santa Claus
under the Christmas tree,
wooden clogs betraying him
like a belled cat.
The legend exploded,
I keep my mouth shut,
use my secret
only to laugh at childhood fools,
conjure the shape of stupidity
whenever my brother talks passionately
of Santa and his elves.

Who'd suspect   hatred

for my next door neighbour
and his mean Dobermans,
when I break each morning
with a hello and a smile,
say nothing of the dog shit
on the lawn, or the rosebush
violated and drooping in the sun?

O silence
how you wear a devil-dancer's mask
and move to the fevered drums;
too often, too often,
you are cracking castanets,
flamenco rhythm
that drowns the true song,
barefooted gypsy girl dancing fire
as if all were right
with the world.

DON'T ASK ME WHAT'S HAPPENING

Don't ask me
what's happening.

I wouldn't know.

Ask me
what happened,
had happened,
and I'll teach you
how to conjugate life
in the perfect tense.

For I have loved,
forgiven, forgotten;
hated

with a white fire in my brain;
blessed   cursed,
laughed and wept
within these four walls.

Seen
the innards
of the heart,
heaven and hell,
here, here,
on this street,
this room, old church
tottering on incense and candlelight.

I have known my God,
adored
when the world was candy and marbles,
questioned, beseeched,
when the dark clouds circled
like vultures.

So, only now am I ready
to let in
the happening thing,
that slice of time
that would dare to balance
on some gypsy's crystal ball,
dance for ever
in the camera's zooming eye.

My past,
those moments of time
I now hold
like a sacrament,
my tempered arguments of living,
epaulettes,
my bloody sword and shield.

(26 March 1995)

ELEGY FOR THE STRAW MAN

About the man
who's cool as an icecube,
likes everybody,
ladies and bitches, old men,
yuppies, policemen on the beat.
An inclusion that smells of politics.

Who's without hard walls, sleek glass,
deadbolted doors
for crowbar or bullets.
He is air, he is water,
a cool pathway open
for anybody/ anything on the roam.

His toys were papier mache,
money cards, tramcar tickets,
GI Joes cut out
from old Christmas wrappings.
There was no solid state here,
no electronic winking,
mechanical wizardry.

So he rides a cool wind,
floats safely on dead sea water.
His life, a small persistent breath,
a smile promiscuous as the morning sun,
an inclusion that seems like strategy,
a survival by default,
a crumb.

Come night, the howling storm,
the maple on fire,
the house under a bulb of lightning,
and he is husk in the wind.

Survival demands
the blood of ordinary men,

those who have seen
the bowels of the storm,
who know the swamp's seductive pummelling,
can find love
in the arms of a lamp post woman,
spit fire in anger, parade

something superbly human,
something surprisingly divine.

4

For The Passionate Ones

and now
the lovers
find
the perfect
glacier
of all
their
once
ambitions

Robert Kroetsch

REQUIEM FOR THE PASSIONATE ONES

Think of those
who mourning their broken poems,
finally took the old poet's advice,
went quietly into the washroom
and slit their throats.

Think kindly,
for this was not cowardice or pablum,
but passion, passion,
the warm blood bubbling
in the final poem.

Think of those
who jumped off the Golden Gate Bridge,
stained a summer sky
with their faithless arms,
limbs hopeless in the air,
architecture
made crooked with despair.

Think kindly,
for they believed the karma
of hurtling arms,
the waters,
nibbhana at the end
of a passionate leap.

Think of those
who buried their heads
in the oven's colourless flame—
how their lungs burst
the blue balloon of their pain,
leaving nothing
but a glaring light
in a sheaf of poems.

Think kindly,

of these who thought the road
never forked,
made absolute the end
before the beginning;
whose lives refused the darkness,
the incessant stoning;
who read death as a synonym for life,
and for one brief moment forgot
the colour of light.

And what are the ways
of passionate lovers ?
I hear weeping
in old Verona, in the noble Houses
of Montague and Capulet.

CRITIQUE IN CRYSTAL

"I've read your book: *Elephant and Ice*
with much interest," says the red-haired coed
to the Sun-Man poet. "I've also seen
your most recent poem: 'The Upside-Down Elephant
Who Would Be a Poet.'
The elephant image seems to rampage
through you work.

"Here's a little something for you,"
handing over a small box
wrapped in sea green paper
with Santa Claus romping all over it.
The silk bow was close
to Indian Ocean blue.
"Thank you," says the poet graciously,
unwrapping the gift quickly
to discover a tiny crystal elephant
basking in the translucent light
of its own body.

Pressing, the poet asks:
"What do you think of my poetry?"
"Look again at the elephant
as it stands on your desk."
He did.

A very lopsided beast
was staring back at him with curious eyes.

NEVER DISCUSS THEOLOGY WITH YOUR GRANDDAUGHTER

Talking about elephants,
how they could communicate with each other
though miles apart, a decibel range
way below the human ear,
my granddaughter interrupts:
Can an elephant turn itself into God?
Well, can he?
No,
but God can become an elephant,
is an elephant,
is the elephant.

Sure. Sure.
Then, my turtle, Happy is God,
and so is Jens's black rabbit, Terminator.
Giggling, she turns
to bury her head in the couch,
and I cannot see the mischief
in her dark laughing eyes, only
sense the shards of my theology
digging into my sweating palms.

SUITCASE

If you mean to ransack my suitcase
for something valuable,
you'll first have to work through
the black bathrobe,
the Viyella socks
(so comforting to the soles
of the feet),
Fruit-of-the-Loom underwear
(passionately conscious
of its mission),
Listerine in Mint, toiletries
that exude "Eternity."

The two shirts and pants
were made in China,
and may well compromise
your sartorial standards.
Almost anonymous
and at the very bottom
is a small white pad
of unwritten poems—
white gold
asking to be mined.

If you are a poet,
your mission should end here,
make your thieving day.
If not, good luck
with the Fruit-of-the-Loom underwear.

NOT FOR HER THE MADNESS OF ART

Yesterday,
          it was penknife against wood,
hard, deep   enough
to make tracks on your mother's dressing table—
that's when I saw her raging
from room to room   swearing the damnation
of child, penknife and art.

I defended your art, saying
good art cuts deep,
               is the only way to learn
true form, how the crooked line
blurs into perfection.

She wasn't convinced.
No sir, not she—
she was into madness,
               the madness
against penknife and child in her boudoir,
jagged lines on snow surfaces,
                    the spilled Chanel,
the oriental doily
               knifed
at the edges.

—OK. So you're now into insignia!
Something to do
          with your insatiable appetite
for Batman.
This time it's yellow Bristol board,
your mother's new scissors,
                    a small bottle
of indelible Indian ink set up
                    on the coffee table,
(if you must know) the cost
                    of the arctic white carpet
under the coffee table is close to

a thousand dollars.

When discovered, my son,
and dire reckoning is at hand,
I suggest
        you surrender peacefully, pleading
childhood ignorance, sheer accident.
You can also try
        your best hang-dog look,
or the inscrutable silence of a stone.
She just might go easier on you.
Whatever you do,
        don't ever serve up
those profound arguments from art.
King Kong rage
        can never understand
the English language, much less
the creative madness of your art.

POETRY READING

(Scarborough College)

Classroom H402,
        way down Scarborough's concrete catacombs;
a hall of learning that suggests
        some soulless architect,
a piece of civilization trapped like an animal.
        And I am here, Pablo Neruda,
with only my fire and my song.

Fluorescent lamps bravely fake the sun,
        pick up faces: young, sceptical, irreverent;
the host professor leans heavily on his cane,
        as he introduces the "Sun-Man Poet."

Not a muscle moves. An audience, cold as concrete,
   is up against my face.

What would you have done, Pablo,
   in this landscape of ice?
Would you have still insisted
   that you were only "a man of bread and fish,"
that you would "not be found among books,
   but with women and men
who have taught you the infinite"?

Yes. I'll fall back on myself,
   ply these rapids with my bamboo oars.
So, I give out my secrets
   word by exotic word,
sing the truth to a rabana beat,
   argue my metaphors of sun,
how the raven can match the eagle in flight,
   the elephant dance on a pinhead!

And   eyes question,
   squint at sun meanings, laugh,
touch darkness, catch fire.
   The Sun-Man Poet reclaims the sun
as applause falls around him
   like a monsoon rain.

GOD TALKS TRAVEL WITH A FIVE-YEAR-OLD
SWEDISH BOMBSHELL

For Deena

Mission accomplished:
her last piece of Lego
sails right over the leather couch,
finds its mark in the fish tank.
Only then does she settle down
to God's simple question:
Deena, how do you go from place to place?
Fast in the idiom of the brat,
comes the answer:
With my legs, stupid!

Swearing something holy
under his breath, God gently protests:
No, my dear Deena,
what I meant was, how do you travel
from place to place, say, from home
to school, or from city to city,
country to country?

Oh! I'm sorry, why didn't you say so
in the first place?
Sometimes in daddy's Toyota,
sometimes in the big blue bus,
or in a big plane
as when we went to visit grandpa in Canada.

OK. So that's all you know about travel?
Yes. What do you expect?
I'm only five years old
and I cannot remember everything!
Of course, my dear. Let me tell you about
some other ways to travel:

on skis, ships (like the *Love Boat*)
trains, snowmobiles, dog sleighs,
horses, donkeys, camels, elephants,
and even by whale belly like Jonah
who made it to Nineveh, or Hababuk
who got to Babylon
in a jiffy by angel wing.

God, God, are you listening?
or if you are hard of hearing
let me know, I can shout like my grandpa.
I have an idea:
since I'm a little bored with Sundsvaal,
can you book a trip for me
by whale belly to Waterloo, Canada?

But God just rolled his sacred eyes
and turned his face to heaven,
leaving a small girl
to answer her own hard questions,
but not without his first catching
the sweet mischief
spilling out of her mouth like honey:

Mean old man,
            must have lost his tongue!

AFTER THE K–W WRITER'S AWARD

The eulogium,
nothing but meat and gravy!

My prize statue catches fire
under the arc lights,

is heavy as brass,
weighs me down like an anchor

as I stagger back
to my front-row seat.

How fame hints at humbling ballasts,
stones at the core.

Why now, Rilke, your voice against victory,
that "to endure is all"?

How this woman sidles up
and asks: "Where are you from?"

Soft baby blues (mask green,
hate, as in hooded clansman)

search for fault lines
in my skin,   black eyes.

Sorry, lady, I have nothing
but the sweetness of silence,

I've already done
with my fire and my song.

HOW TO DANCE IN THIS RAREFIED AIR

How he jabs his thick forefinger
    into my poetic
as if it were a breastbone.
O God, how it hurts;

cups his eyes
    against my passionate burning,
the bougainvillea's profusion,
    elephant
as rogue in heat.

My words, it would seem,
    elude him by a generation;
I would walk only
    in shaded byways or exotic arbours,
the poem jaundiced
    without the blood of a new idiom.

What he wants
    is wasteland:
white, scrubbed, frontier;
    whose poems
must deconstruct to bare bone,
    the flesh and blood laid out separate
to dry like fish
    in the noonday sun.

No; I will not desert
    these wintered killing fields,
the spilled blood sweeter
    among the paddies, the frangipani,
upside-down elephant
    squinting at the sun.
Noble Eliot, you might as well
    rest in peace,
your ransom will not be paid.

My ear to the ground
　　I hear the drumbeat of Avon,
mad Hamlet strut and nurse
　　his eloquent pain;
Milton hammering Lucifer
　　to a superb poetic, a perfect Hell.

Wounded,
　　give me the psalms of David,
words to learn by rote,
　　comfort the dark sargassum
of my days,
　　how the Valley of Death
passes like a bad dream.

I am still here, Montes de Oca,
　　my beautiful wild Mexican bard,
belting my boisterous song;
　　and Pablo, hug me again,
show me the true metaphors
　　of sun and rain,
how to throw my bread on the waters,
　　circle the world with a poem.

Speak to me, Rabindranath,
　　　　I need to hear your distant voice,
bask under your stunning skies,
　　　　and Kahlil, I haven't forgotten
your wisdom that must laugh
　　　　and weep, bow one's head toward a child.

And Dylan, do I ever love the melody
　　of your song, your riotous book of words;
good Manley, sing, sing, sing,
　　I'm all ears and silent;
Lorca, my friend,
　　tell me the secrets of "Duende,"
ask the spirit to stab my words again.

Rilke, take me gently
    into the depths of myself,
the soundless paths,
    how to listen, listen, listen;
as for you, Vallejo,
    teach me the thunder of silence,
the value of the spilled blood,

        how to dance in this rarefied air.